First published in the UK by Sweet Cherry Publishing Limited, 2023
Unit 36, Vulcan House, Vulcan Road, Leicester, LE5 3EF, United Kingdom

Sweet Cherry Europe (Europe address) Nauschgasse 4/3/2 POB 1017 Vienna, WI 1220, Austria

2 4 6 8 10 9 7 5 3 1

ISBN: 978-1-80263-066-4

Crystal Cove:
My Crystal Journal

© Sweet Cherry Publishing Limited, 2023

Text by Sarah Delmege
Illustrations by Paulina Dybała

All rights reserved. No part of this publication may be reproduced or utilised in any form or by any means, electronic or mechanical, including photocopying, recording, or using any information storage and retrieval system, without prior permission in writing from the publisher.

The right of Sarah Delmege to be identified as the author of this work has been asserted by them in accordance with the Copyright, Designs and Patents Act 1988.

www.sweetcherrypublishing.com

Printed and bound in China

Welcome to the magical world of crystals.

This journal is especially for you to explore, doodle, write and discover everything about crystals and how they can help you.

Get ready to smile, sparkle and shine.

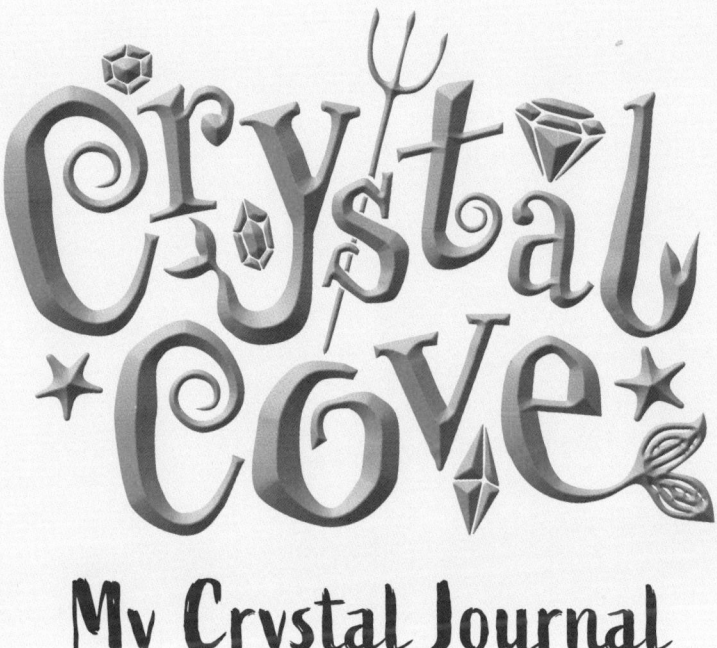

My Crystal Journal

This mindfulness journal belongs to

Sweet Cherry

Contents

All About Me 8
All About Rose Quartz 10
Friendship Checklist 11
Mirror Mirror 12
Spread the Rose Quartz Love 13
Friends Forever 14
You're So You 16
All About Tiger's Eye 18
So Super 19
Confidence Meditation 20
In-Depth Interview 22
Top 10 Things I Like About Me .. 24
All About Amber 26
Wonderful Wishes 28
Letters of Fortune 30
Lucky Crystals 32
Make a Good Fortune Jar 34
All About Amazonite 39

3 Things I'm Going to Stop Worrying About 40
Crystal Colouring 41
Moody Moments 42
War and Peace 43
Breathe It Out 44
All About Angelite 46
Creature Pictures 47
Animal Antics 48
I Spy Nature 50
Which Animal Are You? 52
Delightful Doodles 53
All About Sodalite 54
Are You a Mind-Reader? 56
Find Your Fate 58
Crystal Pick 60
Friendship Predictions 61
The Future 62

All About Fluorite 64	Compliment Cards 89
How Tidy Are You? 65	Kindness Pledge 91
7 Days of Intention 67	All About Turquoise 94
10 Things I'm Going to Sort This Year .. 70	Dream Destination 95
All About Green Jade 72	Enjoy The Journey 96
Bedroom Habits 73	Around the World 98
Your Dreams Revealed 74	Travel Record 100
Sweet Dreams 76	Take a Break 102
Daydream 77	Magical Crystal Washing Water .. 104
All About Orange Calcite 78	Get Creative 105
Crystals LOLs 79	Crazy Colours 106
Don't Worry, Be Happy! 80	Grow Your Own Crystals ... 108
Be Positive 82	Start a Crystal Club 110
Test Your Joke Skills 84	If I Were a Crystal 111
All About Purple Chalcedony 86	My Crystal Diary 112
Kindness Challenge 87	
Kindness Colouring 88	

My favourite crystal looks like this:

I own this number of crystals:

I would like to own this number of crystals:

I believe crystals are magical.
☐ Yes ☐ No

Colour in this crystal using your favourite colour.

What magical powers would your crystals have?

....
....
....
....
....
....

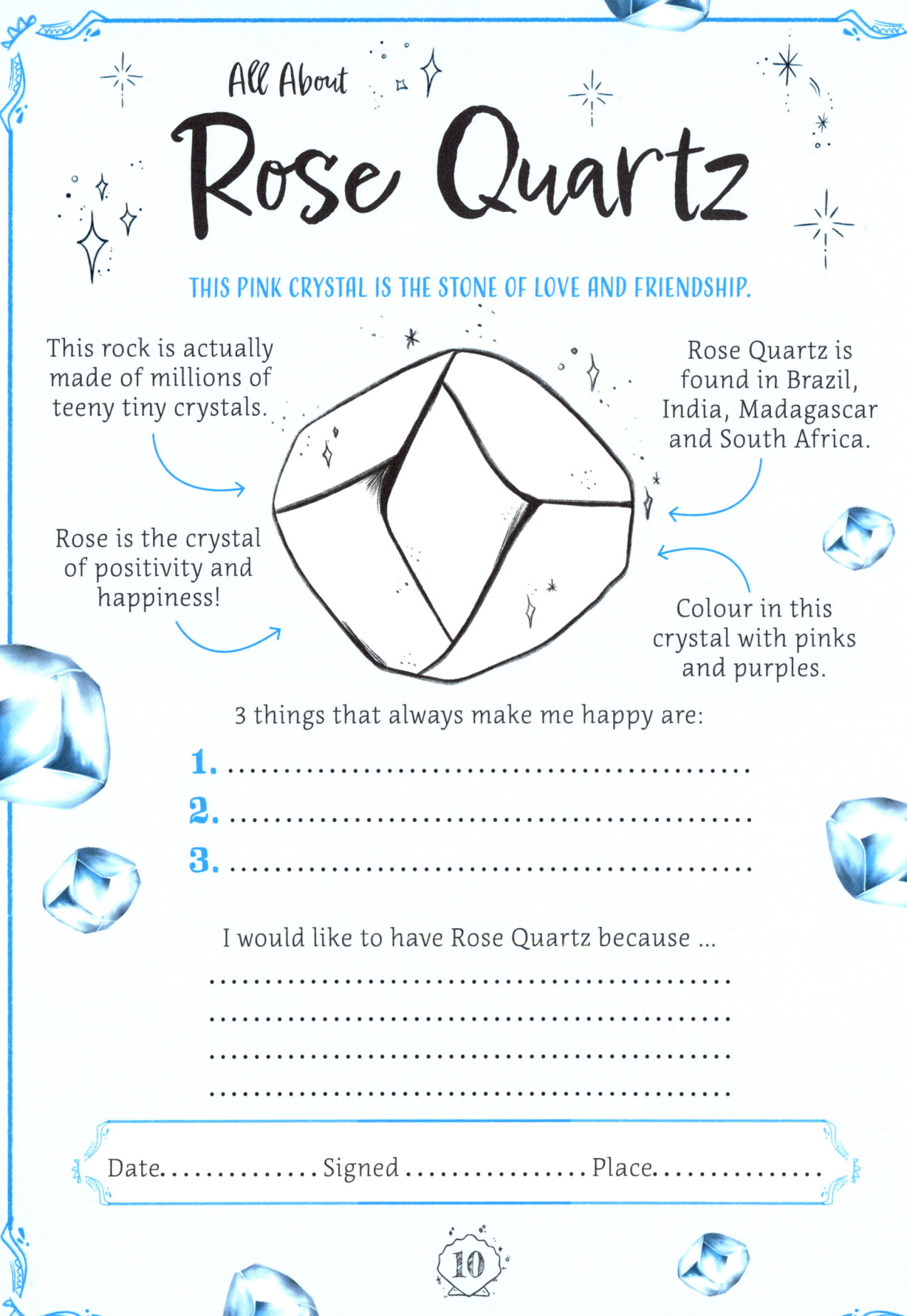

Friendship Checklist

FIND OUT WHAT MAKES A ROSE-QUARTZ-WORTHY FRIEND IN YOUR EYES.

Rank the personality qualities below from **1-5** so you know exactly what you're looking for in a friendship.

1 isn't important and 5 is really important.

	1	2	3	4	5
Funny	○	○	○	○	○
Honest	○	○	○	○	○
Confident	○	○	○	○	○
Loyal	○	○	○	○	○
Caring	○	○	○	○	○
Kind	○	○	○	○	○
Good listener	○	○	○	○	○
Trustworthy	○	○	○	○	○
Positive	○	○	○	○	○
True	○	○	○	○	○

Date................ Signed .... Place ....

Mirror Mirror...

ON THE WALL, WHO'S THE FAIREST OF THEM ALL?

Hint, it's you!

Draw a self-portrait below, then channel the positivity of Rose Quartz and write 3 reasons why you like yourself underneath.

The things I like most about myself are:

1. ....
2. ....
3. ....

Date.............. Signed .... Place ....

Spread the Rose Quartz Love

PICK 1 OF THE CRYSTALS BELOW FOR EACH OF YOUR FRIENDS.

Snow Quartz

This is for: ....
because it will help them think about nice things.

Celestite

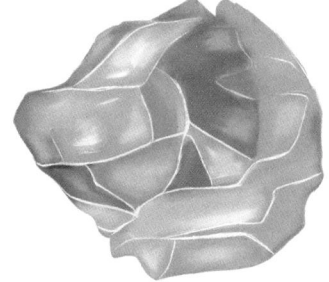

This is for: ....
because it will help them with a creative project.

White Moonstone

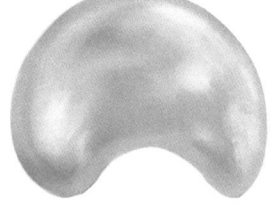

This is for: ....
because it will help them when they feel nervous.

Tangerine Quartz

This is for: ....
because it will help them have a good giggle.

Friends Forever

ARE YOU AND YOUR BFF A MATCH IN ROSE QUARTZ HEAVEN? FIND OUT HERE!

Write both your full names here. (Yours first.)

1. Look at your name. Underneath each letter, write down how many times it occurs in the words BEST FRIENDS.

2. Add up the numbers underneath your name. If you end up with double figures, add the 2 numbers together. So if you get 12, add them up to make 3.

3. Do the same with your friend's name.

4. Put the 2 numbers next to each other. So if you got 7 and your pal got 8, you've got a friendship rating of 78%.

Do all your adding up here!

Read on to find out if you need more Rose Quartz in your friendships ...

0 – 25%
You don't seem to have much in common, but you can still be really good friends as you obviously like each other.

26 – 55%
You may not seem like the best match in the world, but put the effort in and you'll have a fab time together.

51 – 75%
You're a good team, even if you have the odd falling out. After all, it's the making up that counts.

76 – 100%
You love the same stuff, love doing the same things, and you didn't really need to do this test, did you?

Why don't you ... invent a secret language?

Make up a new language that only you and your friends can understand. Try adding *'crystal'* into the middle of every word. Or try speaking backwards.

You're So You

JUST LIKE ROSE QUARTZ, THIS LIST IS BOUND TO CHEER YOU UP!

Ask a close friend to fill in these pages for you, then make a wonderful list about them, too. It's a guaranteed mood-booster.

5 things I love about you

1 ....
2 ....
3 ....
4 ....
5 ....

Written by:
Dated:

5 things I love about you

1 ....
2 ....
3 ....
4 ....
5 ....

Written by:
Dated:

More friends who think you're wonderful?
Tuck their lists into this journal.

Use this space to write whatever you want.

....
....
....
....
....
....
....
....
....
....
....
....
....
....
....
....
....
....
....
....
....
....
....
....
....
....
....

All About Tiger's Eye

THIS GOLD CRYSTAL IS THE STONE OF BRAVERY.

Tiger's Eye is found in South Africa.

This stone is all about being as brave as a tiger.

Tiger's Eye is the stone of focus.

The shimmering light effect you see in this stone is called chatoyancy.

Colour in this crystal using orange.

3 things I need to focus on this year are …

1. ……………………………………………………
2. ……………………………………………………
3. ……………………………………………………

I would like to have Tiger's Eye because …

……………………………………………………
……………………………………………………
……………………………………………………

Date………… Signed ………………… Place……………

So Super

If Tiger's Eye was a superhero what would they look like? Draw your superhero here:

My superhero is called:

....

They are brave because:

....

Confidence Meditation

THIS MEDITATION COULD HELP YOU FEEL MORE CONFIDENT. GIVE IT A TRY.

1 Choose a crystal. This could be Tiger's Eye or whichever crystal you feel most drawn to.

2 When you wake up in the morning, before getting out of bed, sit up, make yourself comfy and hold your crystal in your hand.

3 Take a slow, deep breath in through your nose as you count to 4 in your head. Then slowly breathe out through your mouth, counting to 5 in your head.

4 Repeat this 3 times. Then breathe normally. Say the following words to yourself: 'I'm feeling confident, positive, calm and relaxed. And I feel ready for anything.'

5 Say them over and over again for 2 minutes. Imagine the words are going into the crystal.

6 Keep the crystal with you all day, and any time you feel worried or anxious, hold your crystal or imagine it is helping you to feel more confident.

You can do this meditation every single day and slowly build up the time saying the words to **5 minutes**, then **7 minutes** and finally **10 minutes** at a time. It might be helpful to keep a clock or timer nearby to help you with the timings.

If any other thoughts come into your head while doing the meditation, don't worry, just allow them to flow out and keep saying the positive words.

I first did this meditation on

....

It made me feel

....

Date............ Signed................ Place...............

In-Depth Interview

INTERVIEW THE BRAVEST PERSON YOU KNOW — THEY'RE TIGER'S EYE IRL.

What is your full name?

....

Where and when were you born?

....

Where did you grow up?

....

What do you do?

....

I think you're a very brave person. Would you agree?

◯ Yes   ◯ No

Describe what bravery means to you.

....
....

What advice would you give to other people who aren't as brave?

....
....
....

What do you do if you ever feel anxious or nervous?

....

Who do you most admire?

....

Why?

....
....

What's the best advice you've ever been given?

....
....
....
....
....
....
....
....
....
....
....
....
....
....
....

Top 10 Things I Like About me

USE THIS LIST TO GIVE YOU TIGER'S EYE CONFIDENCE WHENEVER YOU NEED IT.

1.

2.

3.

4.

5.

6.

7.

8.

9.

10.

All About Amber

THIS SPECIAL MINERAL IS THE STONE OF GOOD LUCK.

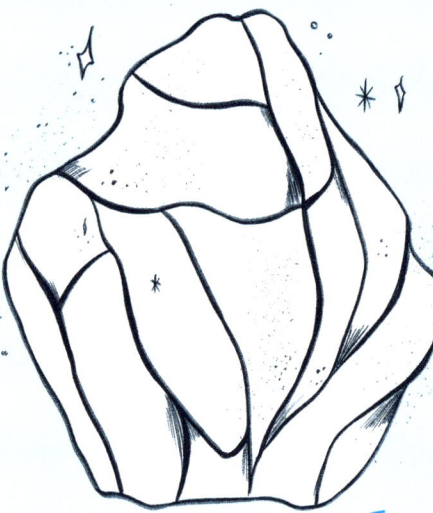

Amber comes from prehistoric trees that are as old as the dinosaurs.

This crystal is supposed to bring you luck as well as make your dreams come true.

It's found mostly in countries that are next to the Baltic Sea, like Poland, Lithuania and Latvia.

Colour in this crystal using orange and yellow.

My biggest dream is …

....
....
....
....
....
....
....

Date............. Signed .... Place...............

Use this space to draw your biggest dream ...

Wonderful Wishes

IT'S YOUR AMBER DAY! A MAGICAL SEAHORSE GRANTS YOU 3 WISHES. WRITE THEM BELOW.

I wish ...

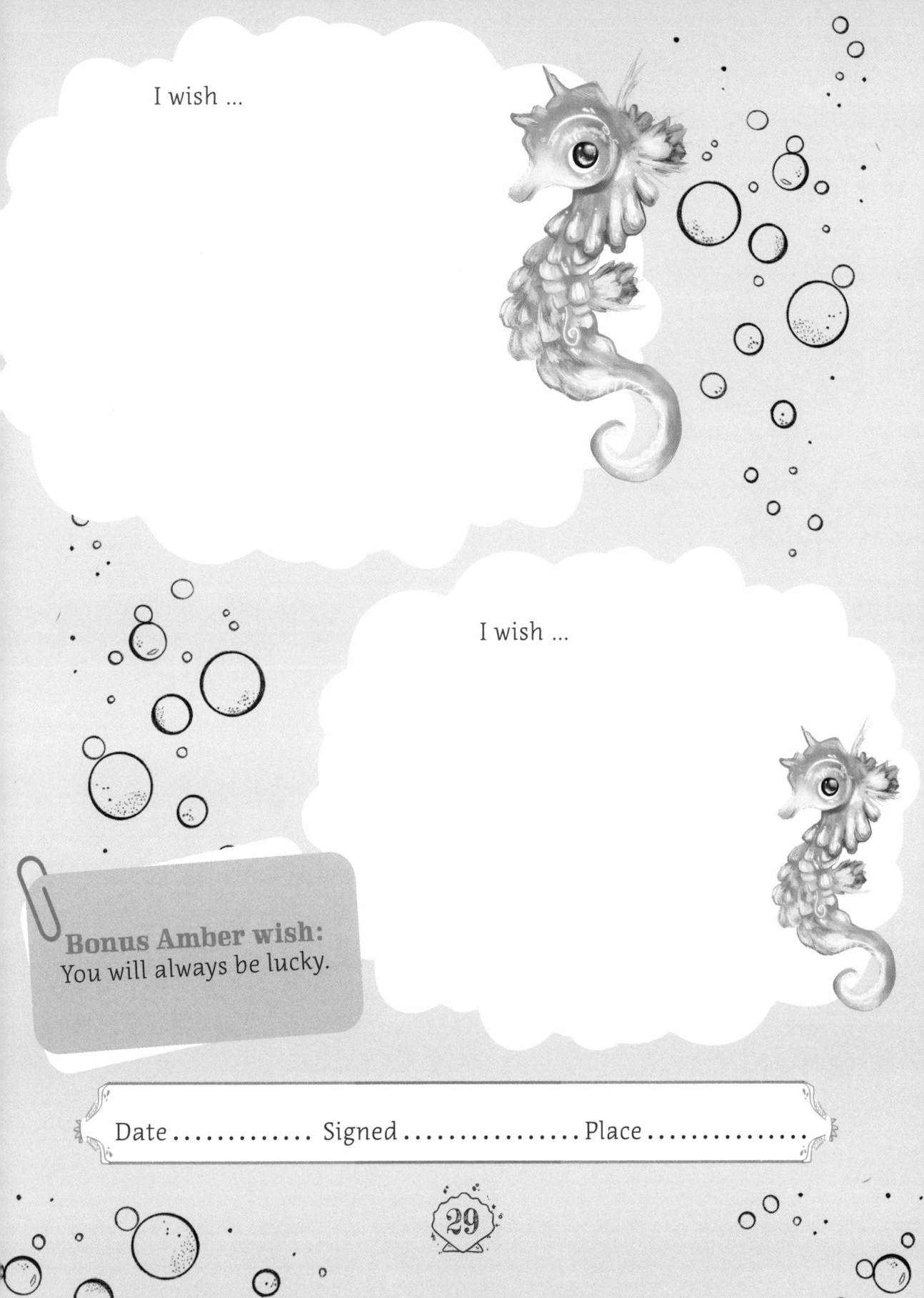

I wish ...

I wish ...

Bonus Amber wish:
You will always be lucky.

Date .... Signed .... Place ....

Letters of Fortune

AMBER IS NOT THE ONLY LUCKY THING AROUND HERE, YOUR NAME CAN BRING GOOD FORTUNE TOO ...

Write down your full name here.

Now, read the description next to each letter of your name. It will build up a picture of what your future might hold.

A You will travel far and achieve your dreams through hard work.

B Learning to think before you speak will be your strength.

C People will look up to your wise attitude wherever you go.

D Risk-taking will lead to riches if you are clever about it.

E Your calmness in situations will always command respect.

F Being part of a team will bring you amazing good fortune.

G Finding friends who share your interests will bring adventures.

H Your secret talent will make you shine in an unexpected way.

I You see the good in others and this is important in your future.

J Use your power to help others and you will always find happiness.

K You will find your soulmate by keeping their secrets safe.

L You care for Planet Earth and will inspire others to do the same.

M Your greatest gift is always making others feel comfortable.

N The future holds great things for you, so stop worrying.

O Loyalty will keep you close to your friends now and forever.

P You're down-to-earth and wise. Don't waste it now or in the future.

Q Use that logical brain to solve any situation that life throws at you.

R Your creative side means there's a lot of fun waiting for you.

S You're great at getting things done. Use it to impress others.

T You're lively and spontaneous, which will bring awesome discoveries.

U Your perfectionism will mean you bring the best out of your friendships.

V You're an individual, so always stand up for whatever you believe in.

W Make sure you think before you leap, and you'll do amazing things.

X Use those daydreams to create something you've always wanted.

Y Listen to other's opinions before making decisions. It will pay off.

Z Understanding what makes people tick will help you get ahead.

Lucky Crystals

ASK YOUR FRIENDS AND FAMILY TO CHANNEL AMBER AND WRITE AMAZING FORTUNES FOR YOU IN THESE CRYSTALS.

This fortune was written by:
....
Date: ....

This fortune was written by:
....
Date: ....

This fortune was written by:
....
Date: ....

This fortune was written by:
....
Date: ....

This fortune was written by:
....
Date: ....

This fortune was written by:
....
Date: ....

This fortune was written by:
....
Date: ....

This fortune was written by:
....
Date: ....

Make a Good Fortune Jar

MAKE EVERY DAY AS LUCKY AS AMBER WITH THESE POSITIVE AFFIRMATIONS.

You will need:
Scissors
Jar with lid
Pen or pencil (optional)

Instructions

1. Cut out the positive affirmations on the opposite page (or write your own in the blank boxes on page 37).

2. Fold them up and put them in your jar.

3. Fish 1 out every day and repeat it to yourself. It will remind you that you can handle everything, lucky day or not.

I am perfect exactly as I am.

My friends like me for who I am.

There is power within me.

I get better every single day.

Today is going to be amazing.

I have a big heart.

I am enough.

I am always doing my best.

I can do anything.

I am beautiful and unique.

Use this page to write your own affirmations.

All About Amazonite

THIS CRYSTAL IS THE STONE OF CALMNESS.

This stone is green to blue-green.

You'll find Amazonite in Brazil, Russia and the USA.

It can soothe and calm you when you feel nervous. and anxious.

Colour this crystal in with the most soothing green you can find.

I want Amazonite because ...

....
....
....
....
....

Date.............. Signed .... Place.................

3 Things I'm Going to Stop Worrying About...

MAKE LIKE AMAZONITE. WRITE YOUR WORRIES IN THESE BUBBLES AND LET THEM FLOAT AWAY.

Crystal Colouring

ALLOW YOUR MIND SOME REST AND ADD SOME COLOUR TO THIS CRYSTAL COLOURING.

Did you know?
Colouring has the ability to relax the fear centre of your brain – the *amygdala*.

Moody Moments

UNLOAD EVERYTHING HERE TO INSTANTLY FEEL BETTER, WITH OR WITHOUT AMAZONITE.

What's your mood right now?

....

Is anything annoying you?

☐ Yes   ☐ No

If yes, what is it?

....
....
....

Is anything worrying you?

☐ Yes   ☐ No

If yes, what is it?

....
....
....

I'm going to make myself feel better by ...

....
....

Date .... Signed .... Place ....

War and Peace

EVEN WITH AMAZONITE IT CAN BE HARD NOT TO ARGUE SOMETIMES. ANSWER THESE WITH A BFF.

A few fights are probably good for a close friendship.

Me   **You**

- [ ] I totally agree [ ]
- [ ] I totally disagree [ ]
- [ ] I'm not sure [ ]

Our worst fight ever was like:

Me   **You**

- [ ] A volcanic eruption [ ]
- [ ] A thunderstorm [ ]
- [ ] A wave crashing [ ]
- [ ] A ripple in a lake [ ]
- [ ] What fight? [ ]

How can you tell when your friend gets really cross?

Me   **You**

- [ ] Their face gets red [ ]
- [ ] They start shouting [ ]
- [ ] They storm off [ ]
- [ ] They go silent [ ]
- [ ] They burst into tears [ ]

It's okay to argue with friends. Just dig deep, find your inner Amazonite and make peace. A friend is someone who knows you completely and loves you anyway.

Still friends forever …
Signed……………………
and……………………
Date……………………
Place……………………

Breathe It Out

THIS MEDITATION CAN HELP YOU SAY GOODBYE TO ANY ANXIOUS FEELINGS.

- Pick up any crystal you feel drawn to. Maybe the colour pops out at you, or it makes you feel calm.

- Find a comfortable place to sit and put your crystal in front of you to look at.

- As you look at your crystal, let all the worries in your head just fly away. Every time a thought or worry comes into your head, just focus on your crystal.

- Keep looking at your crystal and take a deep, slow breath through your nose while counting to 4.

- Slowly breathe out through your mouth as you count to 5 in your head. Repeat this 3 times.

- Now close your eyes and let your breath return to normal. When you feel ready, open your eyes.

Do you feel much better now?

Use this space to write anything you like.

All About Angelite

THIS BLUE CRYSTAL IS THE STONE OF ANIMAL COMMUNICATION.

Angelite is made up of blue and white nodules, which means it has a bumpy, knobbly surface.

This is the Dr Dolittle of stones, and is used to talk and listen to your animal friends.

This crystal can be found in Peru.

I'd like Angelite because …

....
....
....
....
....
....

Date .... Signed .... Place ....

Creature Pictures

DEEP DOWN INSIDE, EACH OF YOUR FRIENDS HAS AN ANIMAL PERSONALITY. DOODLE THEM IN THE CRYSTAL SHAPES BELOW.

Friend's name ....
Why ....
....

Friend's name ....
Why ....
....

Friend's name ....
Why ....
....

Friend's name ....
Why ....
....

Animal Antics

CHANNEL YOUR INNER ANGELITE AND COLOUR ALL THE ANIMALS HIDDEN IN THESE COLOURING PAGES.

I Spy Nature

GET OUTSIDE AND GO FOR A MINDFUL WALK INSPIRED BY ANGELITE.

What did you see?
Draw a beautiful nature doodle on this page and write about it on the next page.

Which Animal Are You?

CLOSE YOUR EYES FOR 3 SECONDS AND IMAGINE ANGELITE IN YOUR MIND. NOW, LOOK AT THE 3 ANIMALS BELOW.

Which are you most drawn to?
There's no right or wrong answer. Trust your instinct!

Jellyfish
You love new people and experiences and are a bright light that draws people in.

Crab
You don't need frivolous things to make you happy. People love you because you're real.

Octopus
You think and act fast. You know that dedication and hard work always pay off.

Delightful Doodles

CREATE MORE DOODLES AND PATTERNS ON THESE CRYSTAL SHAPES, AND COLOUR THEM IN!

All About Sodalite

This is the rock of psychic abilities and insight.

Sodalite is mostly blue, but can be found as white, yellow, red and green.

Its calm energy is meant to tap into your inner wisdom and the world around you.

It was first discovered in Greenland way back in 1811.

Colour in this crystal using your favourite blue.

How psychic are you?

Have you ever ...

- ☐ Known what someone is going to say
- ☐ Felt like you already know someone
- ☐ Found something that was missing
- ☐ Read someone's mind

I would like Sodalite because ....
....
....

Date .... Signed .... Place ....

Use this space to write whatever you like.

....
....
....
....
....
....
....
....
....
....
....
....
....
....
....
....
....
....
....
....
....
....
....
....

Are You a Mind-Reader?

DISCOVER IF YOU HAVE SODALITE-LIKE PSYCHIC POWERS.

You will need: Between 1 and 4 friends

Instructions:
Decide who will start.

Go through the questions one by one, asking each person to visualise their answer in their head.

If the player gets it right, they go on to the next question.

If they get it wrong, the person on their left gets to have a go.

Whoever gets the most answers right, has the best psychic powers.

MIND-READING TIPS:
- Sit opposite whoever's mind you are reading.
- Close your eyes.
- Put 1 hand on top of their head and try to see what they are thinking.
- Focus as hard as you possibly can.
- The answer should pop into your head. Good luck!

Questions:
1. Think of a colour.
2. Think of a sea creature.
3. Think of something magical.
4. Think of a place.
5. Think of an animal.
6. Think of a book.
7. Think of a friend.
8. Think of a grown-up.
9. Think of a flower.
10. Think of a bird.

Write your own list of questions here ...

11. ....
    ....
12. ....
    ....
13. ....
    ....
14. ....
    ....
15. ....
    ....

16. ....
    ....
17. ....
    ....
18. ....
    ....
19. ....
    ....
20. ....
    ....

Find Your Fate

TUNE INTO SODALITE AND GET SOME HANDY INSIGHT!

Draw around your left hand, palm up in the space below. Then add the lines that are on your palms. Read on to find out what it all means.

Draw around your hand here.

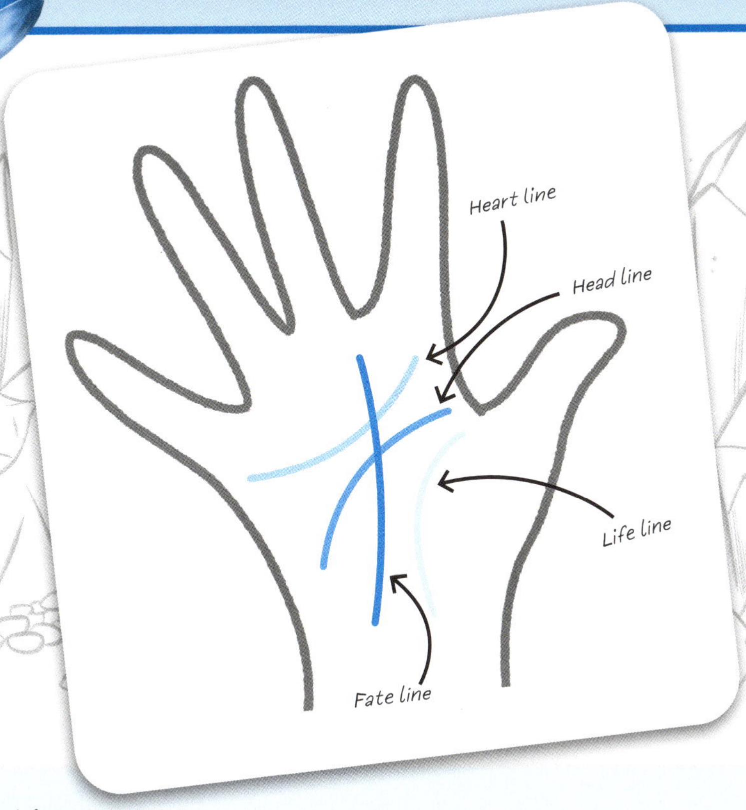

Life Line
If yours is long, it means you're full of zest for life. If yours is short, it means you may have challenges to overcome.

Head Line
If it's long, you are all about being an individual and will always stay on track. If it's short, it means you're very focussed on whatever you're doing.

Heart Line
This describes how comfortable you are meeting new people and making new friends. The longer the line, the more comfortable you are.

Fate Line
If your line is strong, you are ambitious and determined. If your line isn't as long, or you don't have one at all, it means you will be happy with your lot.

Crystal Pick

GET YOUR SODALITE ON AND FIND OUT WHAT YOUR FAVOURITE CRYSTAL MEANS.

Look at the crystals below and see which one you're most drawn to. It could be its colour, its shape or it just speaks to you in some way.

So, what does your chosen crystal mean?

Red Jasper
You're ready for a new project.

Orange Selenite
You're in need of some positive change.

Kunzite
Time to wave those worries goodbye.

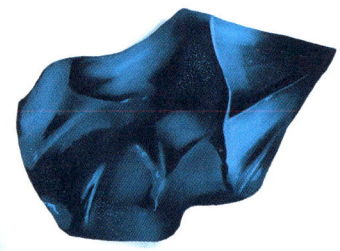

Turquoise
Good luck is heading your way!

Spirit Quartz
A new adventure beckons.

Friendship Predictions

DRAW A QUICK DOODLE OF YOUR FRIENDS AND TUNE INTO THE POWER OF SODALITE AND WRITE DOWN YOUR PREDICTION FOR THEM.

Friend's name ....
Age ....
I predict they will ....
....

Friend's name ....
Age ....
I predict they will ....
....

Friend's name ....
Age ....
I predict they will ....
....

Friend's name ....
Age ....
I predict they will ....
....

Date .... Signed .... Place ....

The Future

PICTURE SODALITE IN YOUR MIND'S EYE, THEN DRAW WHAT YOU THINK THE FUTURE WILL LOOK LIKE IN 50 YEARS.

All About Fluorite

THIS IS THE CRYSTAL OF ORGANISATION.

This crystal is usually shaped like cubes or diamonds.

It can be lots of different colours including purple, clear, blue, green, yellow, brown, pink, red, black and rainbow-coloured.

Fluorite is found world-wide but especially in China, Europe, South Africa and the USA.

Colour in this crystal!

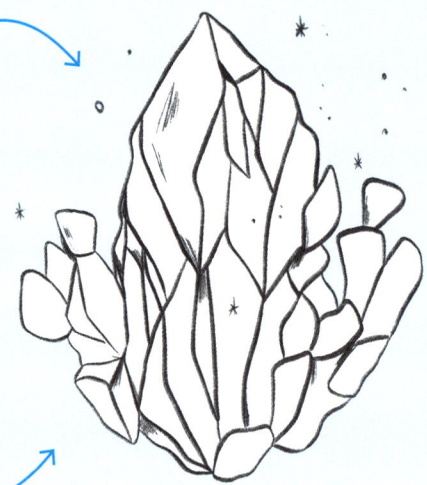

The 3 things I most need to get sorted are:

1 ....
2 ....
3 ....

I'd like Fluorite because ....
....
....
....

Date .... Signed .... Place ....

How Tidy Are You?

FILL IN THIS PAGE TO FIND OUT IF YOU NEED SOME
FLUORITE-TYPE ENERGY IN YOUR LIFE.

If you had to describe your bedroom in 1 word, it would be ...

....

My bed is:
☐ Made   ☐ Unmade

Draw what's under your bed here.

Tidying up is ...
☐ Relaxing   ☐ Boring

Tick every box that applies to your room now.
☐ Used cup   ☐ Dirty plate   ☐ Clothes lying around
☐ Toys on the floor   ☐ Piles of stuff

Describe your dream bedroom.
You can write or draw in the space below ...

Circle the statement you most agree with:

A tidy space is a
tidy mind

Clutter means
I'm creative

Date .... Signed .... Place ....

7 Days of Intention

GET YOUR WEEK ORGANISED CRYSTAL-STYLE.

Each morning, hold a crystal and close your eyes. Now ask your crystal for what you want the coming day to hold. Always make sure it's not too specific or materialistic and nothing nasty!

Write your intention for the day on the calendar over the page.

(If you need more space, you can make your own weekly calendar on a separate piece of paper)

Then write 5 things you're grateful for in the space provided.

Monday

My intention today is...
To smile at everyone I meet.

The 5 things I am grateful for are:
1. *Sweets*
2. *My friends*
3.
4.
5.

Friday

My intention today is...

The 5 things I am grateful for are:
1.
2.

Monday

My intention today is ...

....
....

The 5 things I am grateful for are:

1 ....
2 ....
3 ....
4 ....
5 ....

Tuesday

My intention today is ...

....
....

The 5 things I am grateful for are:

1 ....
2 ....
3 ....
4 ....
5 ....

Friday

My intention today is ...

....
....

The 5 things I am grateful for are:

1 ....
2 ....
3 ....
4 ....
5 ....

Saturday

My intention today is ...

....
....

The 5 things I am grateful for are:

1 ....
2 ....
3 ....
4 ....
5 ....

Wednesday

My intention today is ...
....
....

The 5 things I am grateful for are:

1 ....
2 ....
3 ....
4 ....
5 ....

Thursday

My intention today is ...
....
....

The 5 things I am grateful for are:

1 ....
2 ....
3 ....
4 ....
5 ....

Sunday

My intention today is ...
....
....

The 5 things I am grateful for are:

1 ....
2 ....
3 ....
4 ....
5 ....

Notes

....
....
....
....
....
....
....
....
....
....
....
....
....
....
....

10 Things I'm Going to Sort This Year...

USE THESE CRYSTAL SHAPES TO WRITE DOWN THINGS YOU ARE GOING TO SORT OUT OR EVENTS YOU ARE GOING TO ORGANISE.

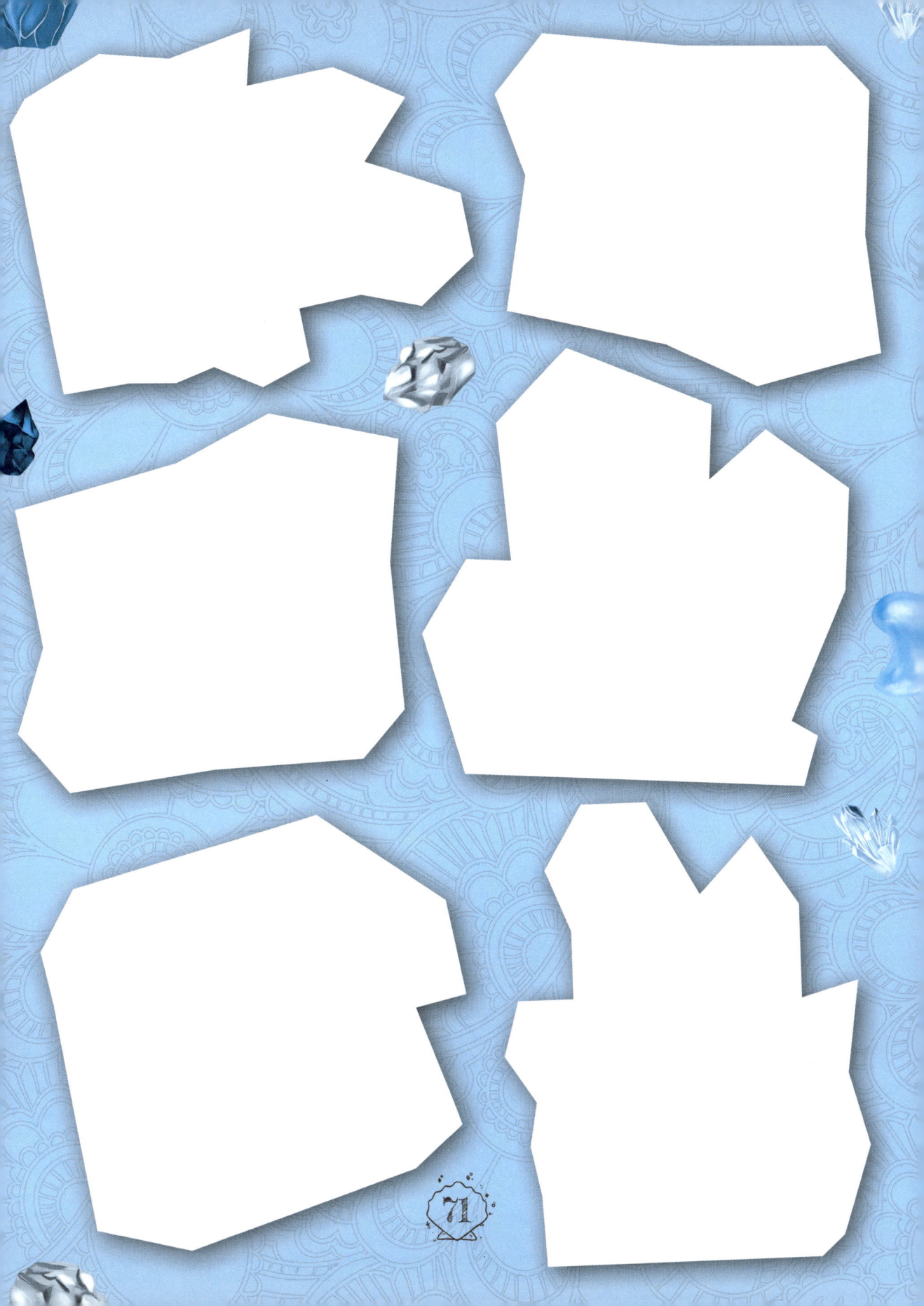

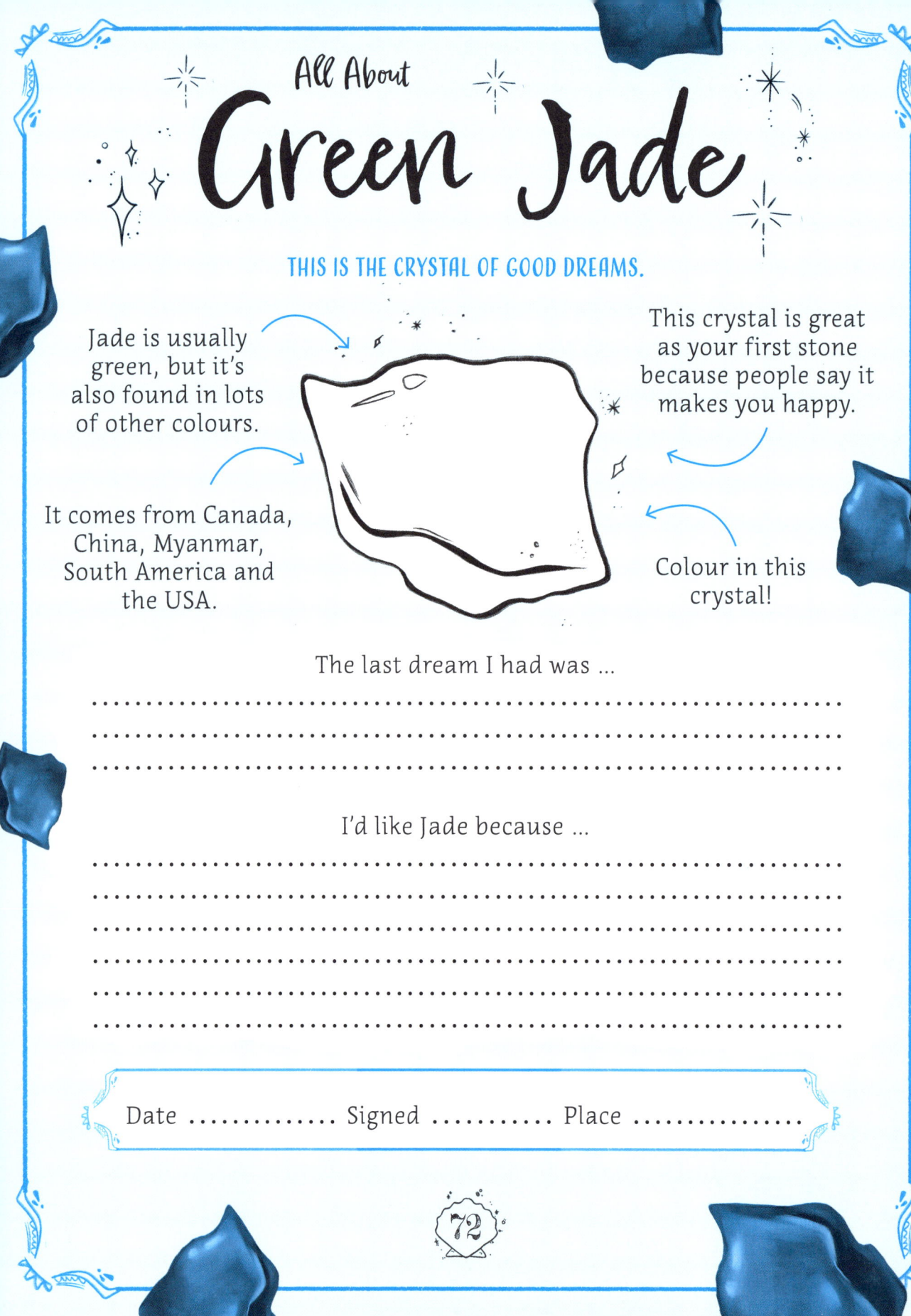

Bedroom Habits

GOOD SLEEPING HABITS CAN MEAN GOOD DREAMS.

Do you share your bedroom?
☐ Yes ☐ No

If yes, who with?
....
....

What colour is your bedding right now?
....
....

Draw your favourite night clothes here.

What time do you go to bed?
....

Do you go straight to sleep?
☐ Yes ☐ No

What do you do if you don't go straight to sleep?
....
....
....
....

Do you ever wake up in the night?
☐ Yes ☐ No

How do you wake up in the morning?
....
....
....
....

Your Dreams Revealed

DID YOU KNOW JADE CAN HELP YOU REMEMBER YOUR DREAMS?

Your dreams are your brain going into overtime, making sense of things that have happened to you. They are revealing your subconscious mind. Here's what they might be saying ...

If you dream of:

An Accident
Oh dear. You've done something you shouldn't have. Don't worry, you can put it right.

Animals
Running from wild animals means you're denying your true feelings. Work out what it is you want.

Birth
You might be about to discover something like a solution to a problem.

Cage
Something is making you feel trapped. Talk to someone you trust.

Colours
Dark, drab colours mean you may be feeling a bit down. Plan something cheery. Bright colours mean you're on top of the world. Enjoy it!

Death
Don't worry, it doesn't mean someone's going to die. It means something is coming to an end.

Fame and Fortune
If you dream of being a star, it might mean that your self-esteem needs a boost. Reach for your good fortune jar.

Eating
You finally understand why a big change has happened or is happening, and you're totally okay with it.

Feelings
These are quite often emotions you're ignoring in real life. Try talking it through with someone.

Gardens
If everything in the garden is beautiful, then the same goes for life right now. If the garden's messy, things are about to get better.

Money
Dreaming of money often means that you're holding back from doing something you really want. Be brave and go for it.

Sweet Dreams

TRY THE BELOW CRYSTAL ACTIVITIES AND SEE IF THEY WORK FOR YOU.

If you have nightmares, say: 'Nightmares be gone' and put **Amethyst** under your pillow.

For lovely dreams, put **Jade** on your bedside table then whisper, 'Good dreams may enter here.'

To remember your dreams put **Blue Calcite** under your pillow, then gently knock your head 3 times on your pillow.

To make your dreams come true, pop **Amber** under your pillow to help, then visualise your dream in your head as hard as you can before falling asleep.

Don't worry if you don't yet have the crystals on this page. Just imagine holding them instead or draw a crystal shape in the spaces above.

Daydream

CHANNEL YOUR INNER JADE AND DRAW THE DREAM YOU WISH YOU COULD COME TRUE HERE.

All About Orange Calcite

THIS CRYSTAL IS THE STONE OF LAUGHTER AND FUN.

This calcite crystal is found as a rock and has a waxy feel when you touch it.

This crystal is said to make its owner feel full of fun.

You'll find Orange Calcite in Mexico.

Colour this crystal orange!

Write the most fun thing you've ever done here:
....
....
....

I would like Orange Calcite because ....
....
....
....
....
....
....

Date .... Signed .... Place ....

Crystal LOLs

MAKE THESE CRYSTALS INTO THE SILLIEST THINGS YOU CAN THINK OF.

Here's an example!

Don't Worry, Be Happy!

THIS SIMPLE CRYSTAL MEDITATION INSTANTLY GIVES YOU HAPPY VIBES.

1 Pick up your crystal. It could be Orange Calcite or any crystal you feel drawn to.

2 Sit on your sofa or upright on your bed with cushions behind you, so you feel comfy. Hold your crystal in your hand and close your eyes.

3 Take a slow, deep breath in through your nose as you count to 4 in your head.

4 Then slowly breathe out through your mouth, counting to 5 in your head.

5 Now breathe normally. Think of a time you had lots of fun and laughed with your friends or family. Maybe you were on holiday on the beach or just having fun at home.

6 Squeeze your crystal and imagine yourself feeling happy and having fun.

7 Imagine stepping into the picture you see in your mind with your family or friends. As you do, you know everything will be okay and you feel so much happier and start to smile. Enjoy being in this lovely place while you're squeezing your crystal.

8 Take 3 deep breaths slowly in through your nose and out through your mouth, and when you're ready, open your eyes.

9 Every time you want to feel happiness just imagine squeezing your crystal and imagine yourself back in this special place having fun.

Be Positive

USE THESE AFFIRMATIONS TO CHANGE NEGATIVE THOUGHTS INTO HAPPY ONES!

What are affirmations?
They're positive words you can say to yourself to change thoughts like 'I can't do this,' into positive ones like 'I can do this,' or 'I'm so worried,' to 'It's going to be okay.' The more you say your positive affirmation, the sooner you'll feel better.

Instructions:

1. Choose the affirmation that you need right now from the opposite page. Take the crystal that matches the words and carry it with you in your school bag and hold it when you need to. Keep it on your nightstand or under your pillow at night.

2. Repeat the affirmation to yourself 5 times while holding the crystal whenever you need to, no matter what time of day. Say the words before you go to sleep, too.

3. Don't worry if you don't have the crystal mentioned on the opposite page. Just pick 1 you feel drawn to instead.

You don't need the crystals to do this, you can draw your own and colour them in too!

'I can do it!'
Quartz

'I can concentrate and focus!'
Fluorite

'I feel happy!'
Orange Calcite

'I want to, I can, and I am going to do it!'
Garnet

'I'm calm and relaxed!'
Amazonite

'I love myself!'
Rose Quartz

'I'm in control'
Falcon's Eye

'It's going to be okay!'
Tourmaline

'I have courage!'
Tiger's Eye

'I feel strong!'
Hematite

Test Your Joke Skills

GUARANTEED TO MAKE YOU GIGGLE, JUST LIKE ORANGE CALCITE!

1. What do you call cheese that doesn't belong to you?
- **A.** Somebody else's Edam
- **B.** A. N. Other's Cheddar
- **C.** Nacho cheese

2. What do elves learn in school?
- **A.** The elf-abet
- **B.** Short division
- **C.** They don't go to school

3. Why do bananas wear sunscreen?
- **A.** Because tan lines look bad
- **B.** Because they peel
- **C.** Because they're smart

4. Why do fish live in salt water?
- **A.** Pepper makes them sneeze
- **B.** Because they do
- **C.** The schools are the best

5. What do cows read in the morning?
- **A.** Nothing. They can't read.
- **B.** The moospaper
- **C.** Pride and Prejudice

HOW DID YOU DO? IF YOU SCORED ...

0 – 1
Oh, dear. Telling jokes isn't your strong point. That doesn't mean you can't laugh at them instead.

2 – 3
You're pretty good at jokes. Take the time to practice a little more and you'll be a champion joke teller.

4 – 5
You're a laugh a minute. You must have everyone constantly cracking up at your awesome joke skills.

Add up your score. Give yourself a point for every joke you got right.

ANSWERS
The correct punchlines are:

1. C - Nacho cheese. **2.** A - The elf-abet. **3.** B - Because they peel. **4.** A - Pepper makes them sneeze. **5.** B - The moospaper

All About Purple Chalcedony

THIS IS THE CRYSTAL OF KINDNESS AND GENEROSITY.

This rock is lavender to violet in colour.

Colour in this crystal purple.

Purple Chalcedony is found in the USA.

I would like Purple Chalcedony because ....
....
....

Write something kind you've done today here ....
....
....

Date .... Signed .... Place ....

Kindness Challenge

THERE'S ALWAYS TIME TO BE KIND. CHANNEL PURPLE CHALCEDONY AND COMPLETE THESE TASKS.

- [ ] Make your bed.
- [ ] Write a letter of appreciation.
- [ ] Draw a picture for someone.
- [ ] Write a thank you note.
- [ ] Make a craft gift.
- [ ] Give out compliments.
- [ ] Help without being asked.
- [ ] Give old toys to charity.
- [ ] Let someone go ahead of you in line.
- [ ] Teach a friend one of your skills.
- [ ] Make a bird feeder.
- [ ] Donate to a food bank.
- [ ] Give old books to a library.
- [ ] Give a crystal to a friend.

Date .... Signed .... Place ....

Compliment Cards

FILL OUT THESE CARDS WITH NAMES OF FRIENDS AND FAMILY AND SPREAD SOME PURPLE CHALCEDONY LOVE.

....
You are one of a kind.

....
I love your sense of humour.

....
You are awesome just the way you are.

....
Your smile lights up any room.

....
You are such a hard worker.

....
You make the world a better place.

....
You're super smart.

....
You're an amazing friend.

Make your own cards!

....
You're the kindest person I know.

....

....

....

You can even cut these out and give them to your friends or family!

Kindness Pledge

READ THE PLEDGE CAREFULLY, THEN SIGN AND DATE.

Remember! By signing you are promising to always be kind.

I .... (write your name here), solemnly pledge to be just like Purple Chalcedony and:

Be encouraging.
Be supportive.
Be positive.
Be helpful.
Be honest.
Be considerate.
Be thankful.
Be responsible.
Be respectful.
Be a good friend.

Date .... Signed .... Place ....

Use these pages to draw and write all the kind things you have done recently.

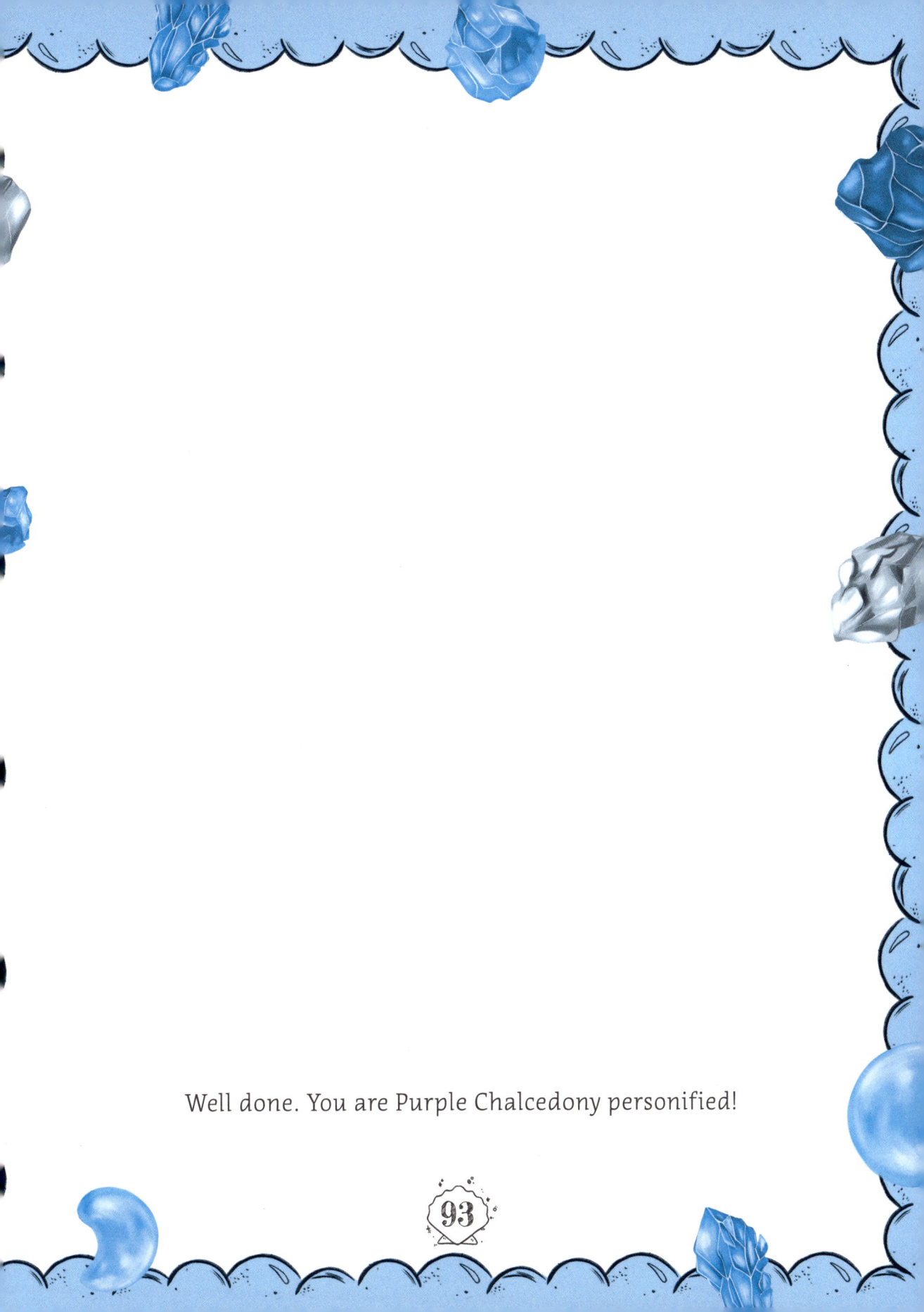

Well done. You are Purple Chalcedony personified!

All About Turquoise

THIS CRYSTAL IS THE STONE OF TRAVELLING.

This stone's colour ranges from blue to green.

Colour this crystal blue-green.

It comes from China, Myanmar, Tibet and the USA.

The longest journey I've ever been on is:
....
....
....
....
....

I would like Turquoise because ....
....
....
....
....

Date .... Signed .... Place ....

Enjoy the Journey

MAKE A LIST OF EVERYTHING YOU NEED TO MAKE ANY JOURNEY THE BEST!

The movie I would watch is:
....

The crystal I would take is:
....

The game I would play is:
....

The book I would read is:
....

The food I would eat is:
....

The drink I would have is:
....

The one thing I couldn't be without on my journey is:
....

Use this page to write even more things you need to make your journey awesome ...

Around the World

BEFORE YOU PACK YOUR TURQUOISE, TEST YOUR TRAVEL KNOWLEDGE WITH THIS TRICKY QUIZ.

1. The Amazon is a big lake.
- ☐ True
- ☐ False

2. Edinburgh is the capital of Scotland.
- ☐ True
- ☐ False

3. It's impossible to sail round the world.
- ☐ True
- ☐ False

4. Canada has a border with the USA.
- ☐ True
- ☐ False

5. There are 11 languages in total spoken around the world.
- ☐ True
- ☐ False

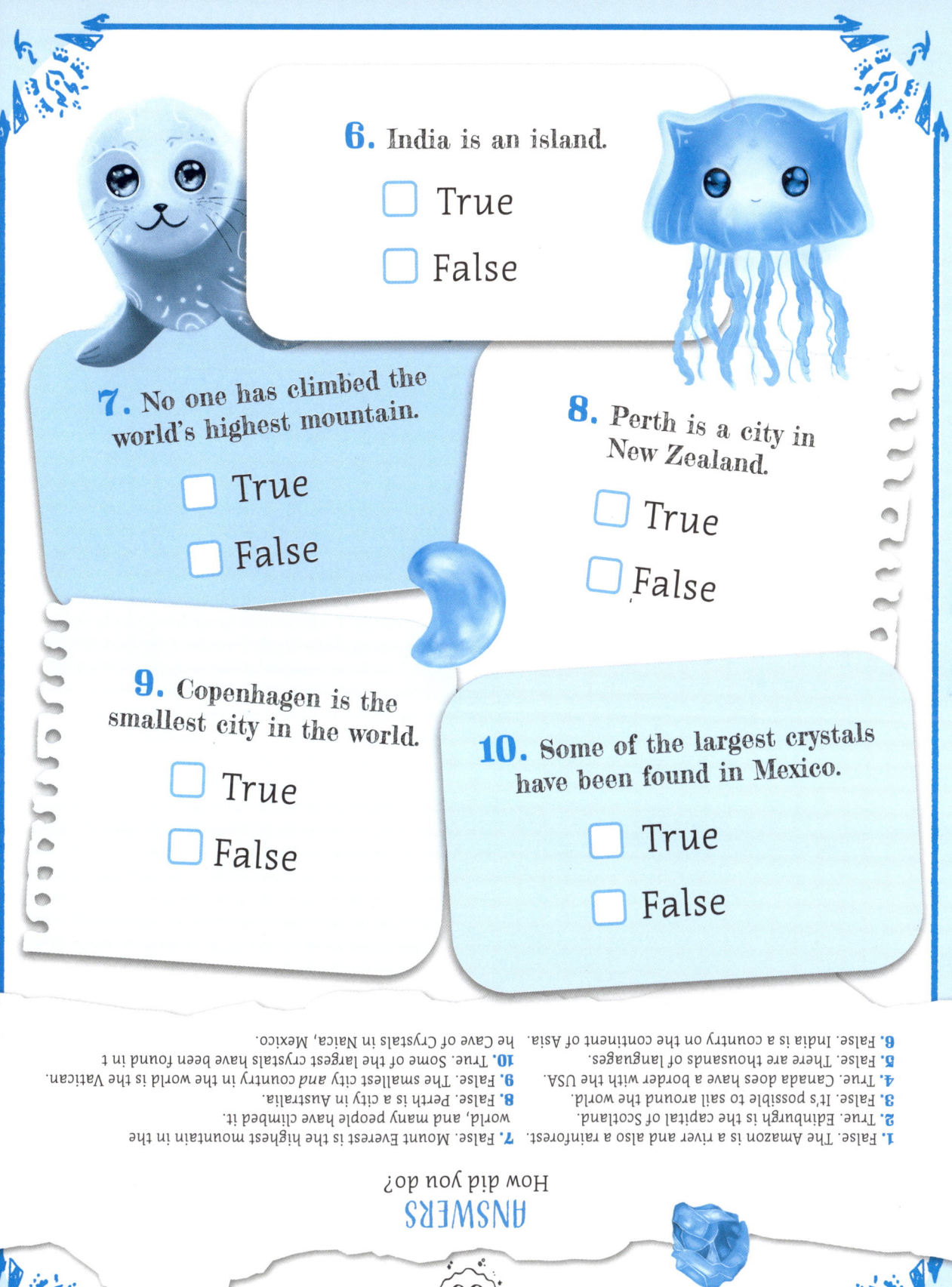

6. India is an island.
- ☐ True
- ☐ False

7. No one has climbed the world's highest mountain.
- ☐ True
- ☐ False

8. Perth is a city in New Zealand.
- ☐ True
- ☐ False

9. Copenhagen is the smallest city in the world.
- ☐ True
- ☐ False

10. Some of the largest crystals have been found in Mexico.
- ☐ True
- ☐ False

ANSWERS
How did you do?

1. False. The Amazon is a river and also a rainforest.
2. True. Edinburgh is the capital of Scotland.
3. False. It's possible to sail around the world.
4. True. Canada does have a border with the USA.
5. False. There are thousands of languages.
6. False. India is a country on the continent of Asia.
7. False. Mount Everest is the highest mountain in the world, and many people have climbed it.
8. False. Perth is a city in Australia.
9. False. The smallest city and country in the world is the Vatican.
10. True. Some of the largest crystals have been found in the Cave of Crystals in Naica, Mexico.

Travel Record

FILL IN THIS PAGE WITH DETAILS OF YOUR AMAZING TRIPS.

What's the earliest you've woken up to travel anywhere?
....

Where is the last place you went on holiday?
....

How long did it take you to get there?
....

How did you get there?
....

Would you go there again?

☐ Yes   ☐ No

Why?
....

What was your favourite way to travel?
....

Why?
....

Which crystal helped you most on your travels?
....

Why?
....
....

Doodle your favourite travel memories here.

Magical Crystal Washing Water

MAKE THIS FUN AND EASY WATER.

Never ever drink this water!

1. Place your crystal in a bowl or jug of water and cover it so nothing else can fall in. Leave it overnight where nothing can touch it. This gives time for the crystal energy to come out of the crystal into the water.

2. In the morning, take the crystal out of the water and use the crystal washing water. Use the water to splash on your face or wash your hair, or even just dab behind your ears to give you good crystal energy all day.

3. Give your crystal a quick rinse with fresh water to cleanse it, then it'll be ready to make another batch of crystal washing water.

These crystals can't be put into water because it will hurt them!

Selenite
Orange Selenite
Peacock Ore
Celestite

Get Creative

WRITE A CRYSTAL POEM HERE!

Fill in the missing sections to make your own, unique poem!

Crystals come in..

They're..

They can help...

It's exciting to choose...

You'll know it's the right one because................................

....

When you feel..

They'll..

Crystals will..

I love them because...

(Continue your poem below if you want to make it longer!)

....

....

....

....

....

Crazy Colours

BRING THESE CRYSTALS TO LIFE WITH YOUR FAVOURITE COLOURS AND PATTERNS.

Grow Your Own Crystals

GROWING YOUR OWN SALT CRYSTALS COULDN'T BE EASIER.

Ask a grown-up to help you with this!
Never touch boiling water without a grown-up around!

You will need:
- [ ] 1 cup boiling hot water
- [ ] 270g table salt
- [ ] 2 teaspoons white vinegar
- [ ] A piece of sponge
- [ ] A shallow dish
- [ ] A container with a lid

Instructions

1. Make your crystal growing mixture by pouring the water, salt and vinegar into the container. Stir until the salt dissolves and you can't see it in the liquid anymore.

2. Place the piece of sponge into the shallow dish. Pour some of the salt-water mixture over the sponge, so it almost covers the bottom of the dish, and the sponge can soak up the liquid. Keep any of the crystal growing mixture that's left over in a sealed container.

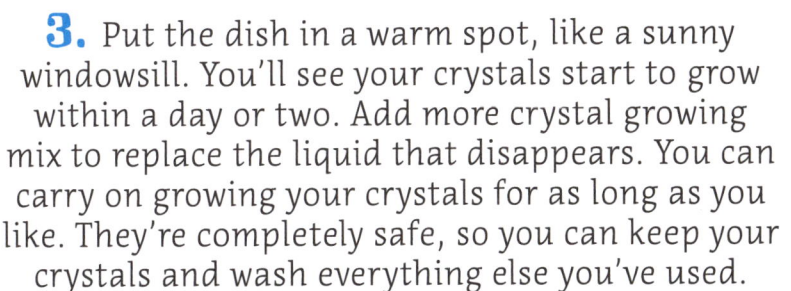

3. Put the dish in a warm spot, like a sunny windowsill. You'll see your crystals start to grow within a day or two. Add more crystal growing mix to replace the liquid that disappears. You can carry on growing your crystals for as long as you like. They're completely safe, so you can keep your crystals and wash everything else you've used.

How do salt crystals grow?

Salt dissolves in hot water, which means the molecules of the salt move apart in the liquid. When you pour the hot mixture over a sponge, the liquid starts to disappear into the air. We call this evaporation – when a liquid is heated and becomes a vapour. When this happens, there is not so much water for the salt molecules to move around in, so they start to come together again and become crystals or crystallise. The salt crystals grow on the sponge, and sometimes they'll grow on the sides of the bowl, too.

I did this experiment on: ....

My salt crystals took this long to grow: ....

They looked like this:

Date .... Signed .... Place ....

Start a Crystal Club

GRAB SOME FRIENDS AND CREATE YOUR OWN CLUB.

My crystal club is called:

....

If we had a badge it would look like this:

The people in the club are:

....

....

....

....

....

....

....

....

....

....

....

....

....

....

Our secret password is:

....

If I Were a Crystal ...

DESCRIBE YOURSELF HERE.

If I were a crystal, I would be the colour ....

My crystal name would be ....

My crystal powers would be ....

I would make the world a better place by ....
....
....
....
....

This is what I would look like:

My Crystal Diary

KEEP TRACK OF ALL THE CRYSTALS YOU HAVE HERE.

Need more space? Continue on separate pieces of paper and slide them into this journal!